THE NEW LIFE LIBRARY
INSTANT CALM

INSTANT CALM

NATURAL WAYS TO REDUCE STRESS

BEVERLEY JOLLANDS

LORENZ BOOKS

First published by Lorenz Books

© Anness Publishing Limited 1998

Lorenz Books is an imprint of
Anness Publishing Limited
Hermes House
88-89 Blackfriars Road
London SE1 8HA

This edition published in the USA by Lorenz Books, Anness Publishing Inc., 27 West 20th Street,
New York, NY 10011; (800) 354-9657

ISBN 1 85967 625 1

A CIP catalogue record for this book is available from the British Library

Publisher: Joanna Lorenz
Editorial Manager: Helen Sudell
Designer: Lilian Lindblom
Photographers: Sue Atkinson, Simon Bottomley, Nick Cole, John Freeman, Michelle Garrett, Alistair Hughes,
Don Last, Lucy Mason, Carin Simon.
Text contributors: Mark Evans, Sue Hawkey, John Hudson, Nitya Lacroix

Publisher's note: The reader should not regard the recommendations, ideas and techniques expressed and described in this
book as substitutes for the advice of a qualified medical practitioner or other qualified professional. Any use to which the
recommendations, ideas and techniques are put is at the reader's sole discretion and risk.

Printed in China

3 5 7 9 10 8 6 4 2

CONTENTS

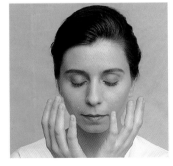

INTRODUCTION

STRESS IS RECOGNIZED as one of the major factors affecting health in modern society. It upsets both mental and physical well-being, and every one of us has felt its grasp at one time or another. Human beings have a wonderful natural system for maintaining balance, and the body is always striving to achieve a state of balance and inner harmony. But this balancing, adaptive energy is tested by stress, and is constantly being challenged. The increasing pace of modern life, the complexity of many professions, juggling the demands of work and family, changes and strains in relationships all place considerable burdens on natural stress-management systems.

Stress is a normal part of life: in fact, a certain amount of stress will do you no harm and is actually essential to motivation and personal development. Some people seem to be able to thrive on it, yet for others the pressure can become too much. The cumulative impact of events sometimes means that, eventually, you cannot go on coping and your body takes the strain.

You can't always avoid stress, but there are plenty of things that you can do to help yourself cope better when life presents a challenge. The first step to improving the situation is to recognize that you are stressed, and to know what your limits are. Taking active steps to reduce the amount of external stress will, of course, be helpful, as well as looking at ways of easing its effects in the long term.

The treatments and exercises described in this book bring together four of the most popular complementary health-promoting therapies – Massage, Aromatherapy, Meditation and Herbalism – to help reduce stress, gain vitality and induce relaxation in a natural way.

Above: Natural therapies such as massage can help you to relax both physically and mentally.

Right: Take time to calm down and allow your body to rest during busy periods of your life.

STRATEGIES FOR COPING WITH STRESS

You can improve your general health and well-being, and thus your defences against illness, by understanding what causes you stress and by learning how to avoid it or adapt to it.

Above: The hectic pace of modern life can make it increasingly difficult to remain calm and relaxed.

A BALANCED LIFESTYLE
There are basically two aspects to stress reduction: lifestyle modification and relaxation. Modifying your lifestyle could mean changing your job and reassessing your goals in life, or simply adopting a more open attitude to what you are doing. Gaining a sense of control over events lessens their stressful impact.

A situation that is causing you unbearable stress can be made easier by asking for help and support from family and friends: talking to someone helps you to see a problem more clearly. Getting regular breaks from a stressful lifestyle will help you to cope better and avoid having a situation reach a crisis point.

Left: However busy you are, making time for yourself is important in enabling you to cope with stress.

SYMPTOMS OF STRESS

The symptoms of stress vary, but if you experience some or all of the following, you may be over-stressed:

- Constantly on edge, with a very short fuse and ready to explode for no real reason.
- Feeling on the verge of tears much of the time.
- Difficulty in concentrating, decision-making or with memory.
- Always tired even after a full night's sleep.
- Sleep itself is disturbed and unrefreshing.
- A feeling of not being able to cope, that it's all too much.
- Poor appetite, or else nibbling food without really being hungry.
- No sense of fun or enjoyment in life.
- Mistrustful of everybody, unable to enjoy company.

Above: Learning the flowing movements of Tai Chi will both relax your muscles and focus your mind.

Left: Meditation can be helpful in calming your mind and helping you through stressful events.

LEARNING TO RELAX

Daily relaxation represents the most important element of maintaining health and vitality. You might try a class in relaxation techniques, Yoga or Tai Chi, or have some professional massage treatments. Deep relaxation is not the same as sleep, and to gain full benefit from therapies such as meditation or massage, it is important not to fall asleep while relaxing. However, you will benefit more from a night's sleep, and awake feeling more refreshed, if you are mentally and physically relaxed before you go to bed.

EXERCISE

A certain amount of physical exercise is important, but take this in a way that you find pleasurable – it could be as simple as a brisk 20-minute walk in the fresh air every day. Exercise not only helps to use up excess adrenalin, but builds up physical and mental stamina. Deeper breathing will supply more oxygen to the brain, which is the first essential nourishment it needs. Daily exercise will help you to relax and sleep properly.

Above and left: Exercising can be fun as well as beneficial.

A HEALTHY DIET

One of the most obvious and successful ways in which we can affect our health is through nutrition. A healthy diet involves eating foods that provide all the nourishment that our bodies need for growth, tissue repair, energy to carry out vital internal processes and to stay fit and active. Try to eat a well-balanced diet rich in fibre, grains and vegetables; cut down on sugar and salt as well as coffee, tea, alcohol and carbonated soft drinks. Three key words are freshness, wholeness and variety. As far as possible make fresh foods the major part of your food intake – fresh fruit and vegetables, freshly cooked bread, pasta and other grains, and a little freshly prepared meat, poultry, fish or other protein-containing foods. Cut back on processed foods as much as you can. Above all, enjoy food: there is a lot of pleasure to be gained from the taste and aromas of a varied diet.

Above: Drink at least two litres of water a day to flush out toxins that build up in the body.

Left: A healthy diet need not be boring if you use variety and imagination in your food preparation.

RELAXING YOUR BODY

MOST PEOPLE TEND TO hold in patterns of tension arising from everyday cares and worries, bad posture and lack of exercise. These patterns make you feel stiff and unbending, and directly interfere with your movements. Inflexibility within the body can in turn affect mental flexibility, and you can become stuck in thought as well as in action.

EXERCISE

Regular exercise not only frees your body, but can also help you to think and act in a less restricted way. Choose forms of exercise that you enjoy and can easily incorporate into your daily routine: walking up and down stairs rather than taking the lift (elevator) is a simple example. Weekend walks, swimming, gardening, cycling or dancing can all help. You may find it helpful to join a class: with exercise like aerobics, low-impact exercises or weight-training, it is essential to make sure that you are doing the movements safely and correctly.

A short daily programme of stretching will strengthen muscles, ligaments and tendons, helping you to walk taller and more gracefully, and increasing your vigour and vitality. For centuries,

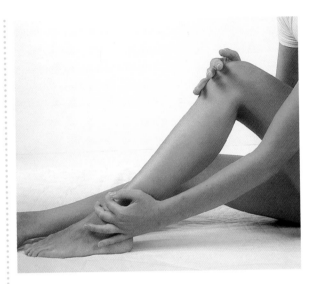

Above: Gentle strokes up the leg aid circulation.

stretching has formed an essential part of the physical exercises that are one aspect of Yoga, the ancient Indian system of self-improvement that embraces the body, mind and spirit. There are Yoga classes in almost every town, and the best way to learn is from a trained, supportive teacher.

Tai Chi is another ancient form of slow, graceful and rhythmic exercise. The movements gently tone and strengthen the organs and muscles, improve circulation and posture, and relax both mind and body. Again, it is important to find a class that you feel comfortable in.

THERAPEUTIC TOUCH

The use of touch to give comfort or to express love is as old as humankind, and is something humans share with animals as an instinctive way of bonding and sharing. Anyone who has experienced the physical tensions that accompany stressful situations will not be surprised to learn that massage is one of the most successful ways to relax those painful, knotted muscles. As a stress-reliever, it is probably without equal.

Massage can have a wonderful effect not only on our muscles but on our whole sense of well-being. Touch is one of the most crucial senses, and the need for human touch remains constant throughout life.

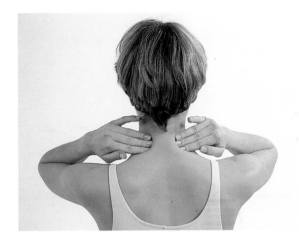

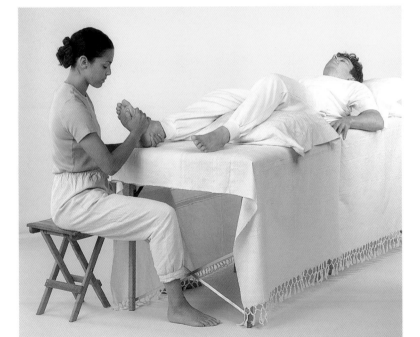

Above: Gentle neck massage provides effective relief for most tension headaches.

Left: Reflexology works to relax muscle tension. During treatment all areas of the feet are stimulated to relax muscles and increase circulation to all parts of the body. The immediate effect of this is to achieve a deep state of relaxation.

LOOSENING-UP EXERCISES

This sequence of loosening-up exercises will be enough on its own to get you more mobile, and will also be helpful to prepare you for more strenuous exercise. Try to breathe freely and comfortably when doing these and any other exercises, and remain aware of your body's response to the movements. If breathing becomes difficult or your heart races, stop, and ask your doctor's advice on suitable exercise.

SHOULDER AND NECK

1 To loosen the shoulders and ease neck tension, try slowly rolling your shoulders in a circle, lifting them right up as they move around, and then dropping them down again.

2 Stretch the neck muscles by slowly dropping your head to the side, towards one shoulder and then the other, repeating three or four times.

3 Then gently swing your head in an arc, from one side across your chest to the other side. Repeat the swing three or four times, keeping control of the movement all the time.

ARMS AND ABDOMEN

1 Swing your arms forwards in large circles to begin to loosen the shoulder joints, then reverse the action and swing them backwards to open up the chest.

2 Facing forwards, twist your arms from one side to the other, letting them move loosely.

3 Continue the movement, allowing your head and trunk to move sideways with the arm swings. Twist right round, keeping your head in line with your arms.

4 Bend sideways from the waist, keeping your hips still and moving your hand down towards your knee. Return to an upright position, then bend to the other side.

5 Extend this movement into a bigger stretch by raising one arm in the air and bending sideways. Repeat the movement in the opposite direction.

BENDING AND SQUATTING

1 With legs about shoulder-width apart, bend forwards as far as you can, keeping your legs straight.

2 Steadily return to the upright position. Repeat the action. If this is difficult, keep the legs slightly bent when bending forward, and gradually work on straightening the legs while leaning forwards.

3 With hands on your head or hips, squat down, keeping your back straight and heels off the ground.

4 Come back to a standing position, rising up on to your toes as you do so. Repeat the exercise several times.

5 Try jogging, running or jumping on the spot (in place).

CAUTION
If you suffer from any back or neck problems, you may be better off with a rebounder (small trampoline) or using a step to go up and down to reduce impact –
get professional advice if you are unsure.

FLOOR EXERCISES

1 To tone and strengthen the abdominal muscles, try sitting on the floor, with knees bent and hands clasped around them. Lean back as far as is comfortable, using your arms to support your weight. Breathe out as you do so and hold for 5 seconds if possible.

2 Repeat at least five times. As your muscles improve, try placing your hands behind your head, so that the abdominal muscles do more work.

3 Get on to all fours on the floor, making sure that your hands are directly below your shoulders, and your knees are in line with your hips. Keep your back and neck in a straight line.

4 Then stretch and arch your back upwards, dropping your head down. Hold this position for a few seconds, then return to the first position. Repeat several times.

CAUTION
If you find you have any pain or discomfort when doing these exercises, get advice. If you find you prefer doing exercises with others, to music or even while singing along yourself, then do so and have fun!

SELF-MASSAGE

Aching, tense muscles are undoubtedly most usually experienced in the neck and shoulders. As you get tired, your posture tends to droop, and the rounded shape makes your neck and shoulders ache even more. Although it is most relaxing to lie down and have someone else massage away the tension, you can massage your shoulders and neck for yourself. Release mounting tension in these areas before your shoulders become permanently hunched up around your ears.

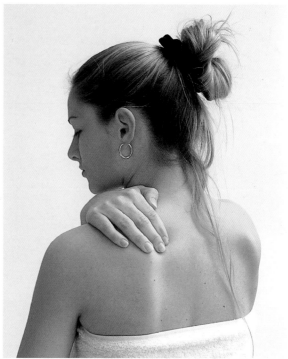

1 Shrug your shoulders and at the same time push them back as far as possible, hold for a count of 5 and then relax completely. Repeat five times.

2 Starting at the top of your arm, knead firmly, moving slowly towards your neck. Repeat the movements in the opposite direction back to the edge of your shoulder. Repeat three times on either side.

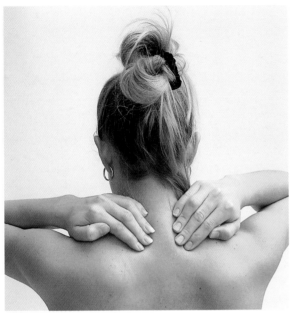

3 Press the back of your neck with the fingers of both hands and move your fingertips in an outward circular motion. Start at your shoulders and work up to the base of the skull. Repeat five times.

4 Gently hold your head and position your thumbs so that they are at the base of the skull. Rotate your thumbs, using moderate pressure. Do ten rotations, rest your arms and then repeat twice more.

Left: Scented candles can add a meditative touch to a room.

Burning aromatherapy oils or scented candles while being massaged provides a pleasantly scented atmosphere to the room and is a wonderful way to relax. The best essential oils to induce relaxation are lavender, chamomile and marjoram. Try not to use the same oil for more than two weeks at a time or you will find it becomes less effective.

MASSAGE WITH A PARTNER

One of the most reliable ways to relax and unwind (you may find your partner drifts off to sleep), a back massage releases much of the tension that accumulates through the day. Make sure there are no draughts in the room and that your partner is warm and comfortable. The oils you are using should be warm and close at hand before you begin so that you do not have to interrupt the session once you have begun. Remember to warm your hands first.

1 Use a smooth, stroking movement downwards with the thumbs on either side of the spine (not pressing on the bones, just outside them) and then take the hands to the side and glide back up to the shoulders. Repeat several times.

When preparing for a massage, make sure you have everything to hand so that you are not interrupted.

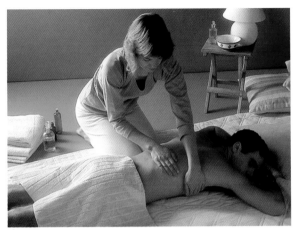

2 From a kneeling position at your partner's side, use the whole of your hands in a smooth stroking movement to pull up steadily, one hand at a time, working all the way up and down one side of the back a few times. Repeat from the other side.

3 Squeeze the muscles from one hand to the other, to knead the muscles of the back and shoulder and release deep-seated tension. Make sure you knead generously rather than using a pinching movement. Repeat on the other side.

4 Stretch the back, using your forearms to glide in opposite directions. Try to keep a constant, steady pressure. Lift the arms off when they reach the neck and buttocks, return to the centre of the back and repeat a few times.

Essential oils should be stored in dark glass dropper bottles in a cool, dark place. Blend only a small quantity of oils at a time to prevent deterioration.

RELAXING YOUR MIND

THE TENSIONS OF MODERN working practices often mean that you are so caught up in meeting all the demands placed upon you that you maintain a high level of mental and physical activity throughout your waking hours.

MEDITATION AND A BUSY WORK LIFE

A busy work schedule means that you are prone to cutting off your emotional responses and your enjoyment of the simple things in life, and pushing your physical and mental health to the limit. To counteract this pressure, you need periods of mental and physical relaxation at different stages in the day. By taking such time out, you will actually gain rather than lose in productivity.

In taking a break every 90 minutes or so, you should aim to change your mind/body state completely. Ideally, stop all work activity and change your physical position (standing rather than sitting, looking into the distance rather than close up, for example) and mental

Above: Meditate in the bath if you have no time elsewhere.
Right: Adopt any position in which you feel at ease.

focus. A 20-minute meditation is ideal, as it is the best form of total relaxation. On returning to work, you will see things afresh and deal with them more efficiently. The feeling of well-being will continue well into the next 90-minute period.

THE BENEFITS OF MEDITATION

Meditation is a pleasant way to gain deep relaxation with time and space to yourself. Just meditating on a regular basis can be beneficial, but using some simple words and images while you meditate can promote an improvement in your general well-being or in a specific area of your life. The mind ceases to be a burden and distraction and instead becomes a tool for paying full attention to the present moment. In this way, meditation practice becomes relevant to real life. The physical benefits include relaxation, improvement of sleeping patterns, lowering of high blood pressure and speedier recovery from fatigue.

BREATHING TO CALM THE MIND

Your breath provides an ever-present and easily accessible focus for concentration: we are always breathing! Concentrating your attention on regular, quiet breathing is both physically calming and helps to clear your mind of any intrusive thoughts as an aid to meditation. Meditation can be as simple as just breathing while sitting.

IMPROVING YOUR RESPIRATORY AWARENESS

Your emotional state is reflected by your breathing patterns. When you are nervous or under strain, you may tend either to hyperventilate (over-breathe) or to inhale short, shallow breaths – a habit that you can only break when your attention is drawn to it. Take stock and examine the way you are breathing: is your breathing pattern regular and steady? If not, take a couple of deep breaths and start again, this time making a conscious effort to breathe steadily. Think about your breathing regularly to check it is still steady.

ALTERNATE NOSTRIL BREATHING

Practise these exercises to become aware of each breath and to help your breathing become more rhythmical and steady. Stop if you feel dizzy.

1 Place the first two fingers of one hand on your forehead, with thumb and third finger reaching down on either side of your nose.

2 Relax your thumb and inhale through that nostril; pinch it closed again, then release the finger to exhale through the other nostril.

3 Breathe in on the same side, then close that nostril and breathe out on the other side. Continue to breathe slowly and steadily through alternate nostrils.

WAYS OF GAINING THE MEDITATIVE STATE

Make a time and space you can call your own and use breathing and relaxation exercises
to ease yourself into the meditative state.

SOUNDS

An effortless sound, repeated with the natural rhythm of breathing, can have the same soothing, mentally liberating effect as the constant natural sound of running water, rustling leaves or a beating heart. The single sound, or "mantra", is used to blot out the chatter of intrusive thoughts, allowing the mind to find repose. The simple, gentle sound "om" or "aum" is sometimes known as the first mantra.

However, the sound need not be a special word; something simple and meaningful will be just as effective. The sound of the word "calm" spoken or thought with each outward breath can work very, very well, especially while imagining tension leaving your body and a calmness developing. Any word that appeals to you will do, repeated with the flow of breath. This clears the mind, slows the breathing and allows relaxation, both mental and physical, to develop.

Above: Repeating a simple sound or word,
such as "aum" or "calm", helps
clear the mind.

TOUCH

You can use your sense of touch in a lulling, soothing way to induce a state of meditation when you are under stress. You can witness young children doing this when they adopt a satisfyingly smooth ribbon or piece of fabric to hold and rub when they are feeling tense.

All over the Middle East, strings of worry beads are rhythmically passed through the fingers at difficult moments to focus the mind and calm anxiety. Their uniform size, gentle round shapes, smooth surfaces and rhythmic, orderly clicking as they are passed from hand to hand all assist the meditative state.

Use one or two smooth, round stones in the same way, passing them from hand to hand, and focusing your concentration on their temperature, shape and surfaces, or find an object with a tactile quality that particularly appeals to you (such as a piece of sculpture) to gently stroke.

MEDITATIONS: GUIDED PROGRAMMES

You may find it helpful to record the following meditation exercises on tape,
so that you can concentrate on gaining the images, or focusing attention, without worrying
about forgetting a passage or having to refer to the page.

THE HAVEN: YOUR OWN SPECIAL PLACE

Once you have managed to achieve complete physical relaxation and calm, allow your mind to enter a place, whether real or imaginary, that is special to you.

Now you can allow your mind to drift...drift to a pleasant, peaceful place. A place where you always feel able to relax...completely. A safe...secure...place where no one...and nothing...can ever bother you.

It may be a place you have visited on holiday, a beach or a place in the countryside. Or it may be a room...a room you have had...a room you do have...or a room you would like to have...an imaginary place. But it is a place where you can always feel able to let go...completely...a haven.

In order to help you imagine this place...notice first the light: is it bright, natural or dim...is there any particular source of light...natural or artificial? Notice also the temperature...hot, warm or cool...and any particular source of heat. Be aware of the colours that surround you...shapes...and textures.

You can just be there...whether sitting, lying or reclining, enjoying the sounds...the smells...the atmosphere...with nobody wanting anything, nobody needing anything and no one expecting or demanding anything from you...you can truly relax.

Left: Sitting on a pretty garden seat can be very restful.

28

Above: Visit your own special place, real or imaginary, where you can be truly safe and relaxed.

A CLOCK TICKING

The hands of a clock record the passage of time – time never stands still, although our perception of time can change. Past – present – future, the clock registers the moments of life moving forward.

The clock ticks...the hands move...so slowly... always moving...seconds tick away. The one just passed is over...a new one takes its place...it too is replaced...as time moves on...each moment lasts only a second. The clock may stop...time...never stops, it moves on...the moment that is over is out of reach... the moment to come has not arrived, yet. This moment is mine...this moment I can use as I wish... I focus on this moment...I influence this moment... I can use this moment...and no other now.

MEDITATION TO REDUCE STRESS

Visualization can be a great help in coping with stress. The imagination can stimulate emotions that can register new attitudes in the mind to provide a powerful influence for improvements in your overall confidence.

Above: While concentrating on relaxing the body, stress and fatigue are dispelled.

THE PROTECTIVE BUBBLE

Imagine yourself in a situation that has in the past caused you to feel stressed or anxious. Picture the situation, and any other people that might have been involved. See yourself there…and notice a slight shimmer of light between yourself and those other people…a sort of bubble around you…a protective bubble that reflects any negative feelings back to them…leaving you able to get on with your tasks... your life, with an inner strength and calmness.

Concentrate on this protective bubble that surrounds and protects you at all times. It will only allow those feelings that are positive and helpful to you to pass through for you to enjoy and build upon. Others may catch stress from each other… negativity, too, can be infectious…but you are protected…you continue to keep things in perspective…and to deal with things calmly and methodically. You are able to see the way forward clearly…solve problems…find ways around difficulties …by using your own inner resources and strengths, born of experience.

Now see yourself talking to someone who has been causing pressure to build. Find yourself knowing just how to let them know that what they are doing, or saying, is unhelpful in resolving the problem or difficulty. Find yourself able to let them know in such a way that they can accept your comments without offence…and find your own calmness and control…a strength that supports you.

You can let someone know if too much is being expected, and explain why. See yourself in that situation…calmly explaining the areas of difficulty…being able to supply examples and information until they understand the position. At all times you are surrounded by that protective bubble of light that keeps you calm and quietly confident, thinking everything through clearly and explaining it simply to others.

Next, imagine pushing out through that same protective bubble emotions that are unhelpful…past resentments…and hurts…embarrassments, too. You push them out through the bubble…where they can no longer limit or harm you. You are now better able to control the way you feel and react. The bubble stays with you, protecting you and and enabling you to remain in control…keeping things in perspective…having the strength to change those things you can change…accept those things you cannot…and move on with more confidence and happiness.

Above: Imagine yourself inside a bubble of calmness and strength protecting you from stress.

Natural Remedies for Stress

One of the main principles of natural medicine is the holistic approach, taking into account the physical, mental, emotional and indeed spiritual well-being of a person when assessing health problems. Physical symptoms of anxiety and stress such as headaches and insomnia, and emotional ones such as depression and mental strain, can all weave together to create disease, or rather, dis-ease – a lack of harmony.

In order to help reduce the impact of stress on the whole system, you need to find ways both to avoid getting over-stressed and to let go of the changes that occur internally under stress. Natural remedies can help in each case.

Aromatherapy

The art of aromatherapy harnesses the pure essences of aromatic plants, flowers and resins to work on the most powerful of the senses to restore the harmony of body and mind. It is well established that scent can evoke memories, change people's moods and make them feel good. Aromatherapy oils can be incorporated into base massage oils, used in baths or evaporated into the air in a burner to improve physical and emotional well-being.

Herbalism

Herbal remedies can also be used to support the nervous system. Herbal remedy plants, known as nervines, aid recovery from stress and are useful when you feel exhausted after illness. They improve the health and functioning of nervous tissue; some act as gentle stimulants while others are slightly sedating. Your choice will depend on whether nervous debility makes you hyperactive and restless or depressed and tired. Herbal remedies are taken in the form of teas, tinctures and decoctions.

Above: The smell of herbs can affect emotions at a very deep level.

Right: Freshly made herbal tea can be a real tonic.

USING ESSENTIAL OILS

Aromatic essential oils may be used in many ways to maintain and restore health, and to improve the quality of life with their scents. Essential oils are concentrated substances and need to be diluted for safety and optimum effect. Treat them with care and respect – and allow them to treat you!

Above: Rose is one of the most complex of all the essential oils, ideal as a general tonic and fortifier.

MIXING OILS FOR MASSAGE

Massage is a wonderful way to use essential oils, diluted in a good base oil. Suitable base oils include sweet almond oil (probably the most versatile and useful), grapeseed, safflower, soya (a bit thicker and stickier), coconut and even sunflower. For very dry skins, a small amount of jojoba, avocado or wheat germ oils (except in cases of wheat allergy) may be added. Blend essential oils at a dilution of 1 per cent, or one drop per 5 ml/1 tsp base oil; this may sometimes be increased to 2 per cent, but take care that no skin reactions occur with any oil.

CAUTION
• Never take essential oils internally, unless professionally prescribed.
• Always use essential oils diluted – normally 1 per cent for massage; just 5 drops in a bath or for a steam inhalation.
• Do not use the same oils for too long: follow the "1–2 rule"; use one or two oils together, for not more than one or two weeks at any one time.
• Do not use oils in pregnancy, without getting professional advice; some oils, such as basil, clary sage, juniper, marjoram and sage, are contra-indicated at this time.

Above: Get your partner to massage you with a relaxing blend of essential oils as the perfect antidote to an overdose of life's stresses.

SCENTED ROOMS

You can create an aromatic environment, at home or in the workplace, by using essential oils in a vaporizer to disperse their beneficial aromas into the air. They can help to prevent ill-health and to balance the emotions, as well as freshening the atmosphere.

Rose, geranium, orange and lavender are pleasing and uplifting scents for a living room, used individually or blended together; bergamot is an excellent anti-depressant. At work, lemon helps efficiency while rosemary is a great aid to concentration.

BATHS

Soak in a warm bath, enveloped in delicious scent, and feel all the day's tensions melt away. Pour in 5 drops of your chosen blend just before you get into the water. The oils will be partly absorbed by your skin while you breathe in the scent, producing an immediate psychological and physiological effect.
• For a refreshing, uplifting morning bath, blend 3 drops bergamot and 2 drops geranium.
• To relax and unwind after a long day, blend 3 drops lavender and 2 drops ylang ylang.
• For tired, tense muscles, blend 3 drops marjoram and 2 drops chamomile.

Above: Lavender-scented candles can be relaxing.

RELAXING AND UPLIFTING ESSENTIAL OILS

Essential oils may be extracted from exotic plants such as sandalwood or ylang ylang, or from more common plants like lavender and chamomile, but each one has its own characteristics and properties. For the best results, use only the finest oils, bought from a reputable source.

BERGAMOT (*Citrus bergamia*)
The peel of the ripe fruit yields an oil that is mild and gentle. It is the most effective antidepressant of all, best used at the start of the day. Do not use on the skin before going into bright sunlight, as it increases photosensitivity.

CHAMOMILE (*Chamomilla recutita*)
Chamomile is relaxing and antispasmodic, helping to relieve tension headaches, nervous digestive problems and insomnia.

CLARY SAGE (*Salvia sclarea*)
This oil gives a definite euphoric uplift to the brain; do not use too much, however, as you can be left feeling very spacey! Like ylang ylang and jasmine, its antidepressant and relaxing qualities have contributed to its reputation as an aphrodisiac.

FRANKINCENSE (*Boswellia thurifera*)
The essence is spicy, with undertones of camphor, but becomes lemony when mixed with myrrh. It also blends well with sandalwood. Frankincense is warming and relaxing and is an excellent aid to meditation, as it deepens and slows the breath.

GERANIUM (*Pelargonium graveolens*)
The rose-scented geranium has very useful properties, not least being its ability to bring a blend together to make a more harmonious scent. Geranium has a refreshing, antidepressant quality, good for nervous tension and exhaustion.

JASMINE (*Jasminum officinale*)
An ancient favourite of the Arabs, Indians and Chinese, jasmine has a wonderful aroma with a relaxing, euphoric effect. It can greatly lift the mood when there is debility, depression and listlessness.

LAVENDER (*Lavandula angustifolia/officinalis*)
One of the safest and most versatile of all essential oils, lavender has been used for centuries as a refreshing fragrance and as a remedy for stress-related ailments. It is especially helpful for tension headaches or for nervous digestive systems. Use in a massage blend or in the bath for a deeply relaxing and calming experience.

LEMON (*Citrus limon*)
Possibly the most cleansing
and antiseptic of the citrus
oils, useful for boosting the immune
system and in skin care. It can also
refresh and clarify thoughts.

MARJORAM (*Origanum majorana*)
Marjoram has a calming, warming effect, and is good
for both cold, tight muscles and for cold, tense people
who may suffer from headaches, migraines and
insomnia. Use in massage blends for tired, aching
muscles, or in the bath, especially in the evening to
encourage a good night's sleep.

NEROLI (*Citrus aurantium*)
Neroli is one of the finest of the floral essences. Its
effect is uplifting and calming, bringing a feeling of
peace. It is useful during times of anxiety, panic,
hysteria or shock and fear. It can help in the development of self-esteem and is particularly effective for
nervous diarrhoea and other stress-related conditions.

ORANGE (*Citrus aurantium*)
Refreshing but sedative, orange is
a tonic for anxiety and depression,
having a similar effect to neroli,
which is distilled from the
blossom of the same plant. Orange
also stimulates the digestive system
and is effective for constipation.
Because the oil oxidizes
very quickly, it cannot be kept
for very long.

ROSE (*Rosa* x *damascena trigintipetala*)
The scent evokes a general sense
of pleasure and happiness. The
actions of the oil are sedating,
calming and anti-inflammatory.
Not surprisingly, rose oil has a
wide reputation as an aphrodisiac,
and where anxiety is a factor it
can be very beneficial. Add to a base massage oil to
soothe muscular and nervous tension.

ROSEMARY (*Rosmarinus officinalis*)
With a very penetrating, stimulating aroma, rosemary
has been used for centuries to help relieve nervous
exhaustion, tension headaches and migraines. It
improves circulation to the brain and is an excellent
oil for mental fatigue and debility. Avoid in cases of
high blood pressure. Pregnant women should also
avoid rosemary oil as it stimulates the uterus and can
cause miscarriage.

SANDALWOOD (*Santalum album*)
Probably the oldest perfume in history, sandalwood is
known to have been used for over 4,000 years. It has a
relaxing, antidepressant effect on the nervous system,
and where depression causes sexual problems sandalwood can be a genuine aphrodisiac.

YLANG YLANG (*Cananga odorata*)
This intensely sweet essential oil has a sedative yet
antidepressant action. It is good for many symptoms
of excessive tension, such as insomnia, panic attacks,
anxiety and depression. It also has a reputation as an
aphrodisiac, through its ability to reduce stress levels.

PREPARING HERBAL REMEDIES

There is much you can do with herbs to treat minor health problems and help your body deal with stress. Getting to know the plants growing around you can be a relaxing pleasure in itself, and if you learn about their various properties you can use them to help you feel better able to cope with everyday problems.

USING HERBS

If you grow herbs in your garden they can be used fresh or harvested when they are abundant and dried for future use. Many herbs are, of course, a delicious addition to food, or they can be taken internally in a variety of other forms: as teas, decoctions, tinctures, inhalations, capsules and powders. Externally, herbs can be applied as compresses, poultices, ointments or infused oils. You can also add fresh herbs or herbal oils to your bath for a therapeutic soak.

MAKING HERBAL TEAS

You can use either fresh or dried herbs to make a tea (use twice as much fresh material as dried). If you find the taste of some herb teas unpleasant, they can be sweetened with a little honey or flavoured by stirring with a licorice stick or adding slices of fresh ginger.

1 Put your chosen herb or herbs into a teapot with a close-fitting lid. A standard-strength tea is made with 5 ml/1 tsp dried or 10 ml/2 tsp fresh herbs to each cup of water. Add boiling water, cover and leave to steep for 10–15 minutes.

2 Strain and drink as required. Teas can be drunk hot or cold, and can be re-heated. They will keep, covered, in the fridge for up to 24 hours.

MAKING TINCTURES

Sometimes it is more convenient to take a spoonful of medicine, or place a few drops of a tincture on your tongue, rather than drinking tea. Tinctures are made by steeping herbs in a mixture of alcohol and water. The alcohol extracts the medicinal constituents and also acts as a preservative.

1 Place 100 g/4 oz dried herbs or 300 g/11 oz fresh herbs in a jar.

2 Mix 120 ml/4 fl oz/½ cup vodka (30% alcohol, or 60° proof) with 350 ml/12 fl oz/1½ cups water and add to the herbs.

3 Leave the herbs to steep in the liquid for a month, preferably on a sunny windowsill. Gently shake the jar every day.

4 Strain and store the tincture in a dark glass bottle (it will keep for up to 18 months).

RELAXING AND UPLIFTING HERBS

These herbs are particularly useful for managing stress and its symptoms. Herbs do not usually work instantly, so give them at least two weeks to begin to take effect. Select a remedy that suits your symptoms: if when under stress you feel depressed, you should look for a stimulating tonic such as wild oats or St John's wort. If, however, stress makes you anxious, with symptoms such as palpitations, sweating and sleeplessness, turn towards relaxing herbs like skullcap or vervain.

BORAGE (*Borago officinalis*)
Traditionally associated with courage, borage improves the production of adrenalin and is therefore useful during stressful times. It is commercially available in capsules and is sometimes called starflower oil.

CHAMOMILE (*Chamomilla recutita*)
Use the flowerheads alone in a tea or tincture to relax both the digestive function and gut feelings which may sometimes disturb you. It makes a fine after-dinner drink, as it also promotes a feeling of relaxation. Chamomile tea-bags are useful and convenient (they can be bought at health food stores and some supermarkets), but an infusion of loose flowers usually makes a better quality tea.

LAVENDER (*Lavandula angustifolia*)
Lavender can be taken in a tincture or tea (use 2.5 ml/½ tsp to a cup of boiling water three times a day), and the flowers can be used to flavour biscuits (cook-

ies), vinegar, desserts and ice creams. It is an ideal remedy for irritation, indigestion and potential migraines. A few fresh or dried flowers added to teas made with other herbs will have a cheering effect.

LEMON BALM (*Melissa officinalis*)
This is one of the few herbs that don't keep their flavour on drying, so pick it fresh daily and freeze some for winter. It is often used for irritable bowel, nervous

indigestion, anxiety and depression. Drinking lemon balm tea also encourages a clear head, so it is useful when you are studying. It makes a good bedtime drink, promoting peaceful sleep and relaxation.

St John's wort (*Hypericum perforatum*)

Traditionally, St John's wort was considered to be magically protective and a remedy for melancholy. It is now becoming well known for its antidepressant action. It is a nerve tonic that helps both nervous exhaustion and damage to nerves caused by diseases such as herpes and shingles. The flowering tops are made into a tea, using 5 ml/1 tsp dried or 10 ml/ 2 tsp fresh herb to a cup of boiling water: drink three times a day.

Skullcap (*Scutellaria lateriflora*)

This nerve tonic is very calming, having the same effect as a gentle hand placed comfortingly on the head. Skullcap can help the anxiety and restlessness that often accompany an overload of worries or responsibilities. The aerial parts of the plant should be harvested after flowering. Use 5 ml/1 tsp dried or 10ml/2 tsp fresh herb to a cup of boiling water.

Vervain (*Verbena officinalis*)

Vervain is a nerve tonic with a slightly sedative action. It is useful for nervous exhaustion and symptoms of tension which include headaches and nausea – migraines, for example. It is also recommended for depression and combines well with oats. Disguise the bitter taste by sweetening the tea with a little honey.

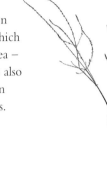

Wild oats (*Avena sativa*)

Oats are an excellent tonic to the nervous system, giving both nourishment and energy. They are slightly stimulating and a long-term remedy for nervous exhaustion, lifting the mood while improving adaptability. They can be eaten in porridge, flapjacks, oatcakes and other dishes, but should be avoided if you are sensitive to gluten.

Wood betony (*Stachys betonica*)

An attractive plant with purple flowers growing out of a satisfying cushion of leaves, betony restores the nervous system, especially if sick headaches and poor memory are a problem. It has the effect of  encouraging blood flow to the head. Avoid high doses in pregnancy.

RELIEVING THE SYMPTOMS OF STRESS

THE INVOLUNTARY OR autonomic nervous system has two divisions. The parasympathetic system is responsible for the body's "housekeeping", ensuring good digestion, assimilation of nutrients, detoxification and elimination of waste products. The sympathetic part prepares you for action and initiates the "fight or flight" response – making the heart and lungs more active and suppressing processes such as digestion and elimination. These mechanisms were originally developed to cope with potentially life-threatening situations, but nowadays are all too often brought into play by other factors, from meeting deadlines to receiving a stack of bills to pay.

If you are subject to too much stimulation, sympathetic activities become dominant or habitual and may reach a state of exhaustion, reducing your ability to react to new stresses that may arise. This stressed state can cause forgetfulness, panic, insomnia, exhaustion or vulnerability to infection. The converse problem is reduced parasympathetic activity, which can cause all sorts of digestive and nutritional debilities as well as poor elimination, resulting in problems with the skin, muscles or joints.

So stress can give rise to a host of physical as well as emotional problems, which will in turn weaken your body's performance and therefore your ability to cope with everyday pressure. Stressful events are likely to disrupt your appetite and your ability to rest, but both are vital to enable you to cope well. Natural therapies can offer help with many stress-related problems, to help you escape this vicious cycle and come through a difficult time.

Above: A hot bath, calming herbal tea and a book to read can all work wonders on your stress levels.

Right: Steam inhalations can be deeply relaxing and soothing.

REDUCING TENSION HEADACHES

Headaches are a common symptom of stress. Often they are caused by tension in the neck and upper back muscles. This can prevent adequate blood supply to the head and thus lead to pain. Both massage and exercise can be a great help in easing this kind of headache.

SHIATSU FOR HEADACHE RELIEF

1 Seat your partner on an upright chair that has good back support. Stand behind your partner and place both hands loosely on either side of your partner's neck. Gently massage the shoulders to help relax the breathing and create a feeling of well-being.

2 Tilt the head to the side and support with the palm of your hand so that the neck muscles can relax. Place the forearm across the shoulder and slowly apply gentle downward pressure. Hold for 5–10 seconds, then repeat for the other side.

3 Supporting the head, apply gentle pressure with the thumb and forefinger from the base of the neck to the nape. Hold at the nape of the neck for 5 seconds and then release.

Tilt the head back slightly, supporting it on your chest. Place your thumbs on the temples with the fingers resting on either side of the face. Rotate the thumbs in small forward movements.

4 Find the pressure points just above the inner corner of each eye. Apply gentle pressure with the middle fingers to help disperse the pain. Hold for 5 seconds.

5 Position your thumbs about 5 cm/2 in apart on either side of the head just above the hairline, with the palms pressed flat along the sides of the face. Press the thumbs evenly back along the top of the head.

SOOTHING TEA
Put 5 ml/1 tsp dried wood betony and 2.5 ml/½ tsp dried lavender or rosemary into a cup. Top up with boiling water and leave to steep for 10 minutes. Strain and drink. Repeat hourly throughout the day.

Above: Wood betony.

LAVENDER OR ROSEMARY SCENTED BATH
Pour a few drops of lavender or rosemary essential oil into a hot bath. Even better, tie a bunch of the fresh herb under the hot tap as you fill the bath, or fill a muslin bag with dried herbs to scent the water.

Left: Soak away the day's tension with a scented bath.

INSTANT REVITALIZERS

Chronic tension all too often leads to a feeling of exhaustion, when you just run out of steam. When you need to be bright and alert before an important meeting, a long drive or a party, try these simple exercises to give you that instant tonic to set you on your feet again.

SELF-MASSAGE: ARMS, SHOULDERS AND NECK

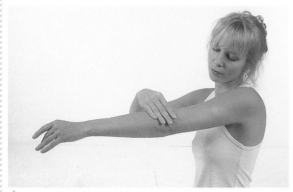

1 Do a kneading action on the arms, working rapidly from the wrist to the shoulder and back again with a firm squeezing movement.

2 Rub swiftly up the outside of each arm to stimulate the circulation. Work in an upwards direction each time to encourage blood flow back to the heart.

3 With the fingers and thumb of one hand, firmly squeeze the neck muscles, using a circular motion.

Above: Mandarin oil is very invigorating.

SELF-MASSAGE: LEGS AND BUTTOCKS

1 Sitting down, with one leg raised slightly, stroke the leg with both hands from ankle to thigh. Begin the stroke as close to the ankle as you can reach. Repeat several times, moving around the leg slightly each time to stroke a different part.

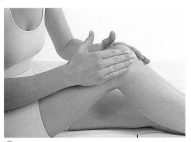

2 Massage the knee, slowly stroking around the outside of the kneecap to begin with, then using circular pressure with the finger-tips to work around the kneecap more firmly.

3 Knead the calf muscle with both hands, using a firm *pétrissage* (squeezing action) to loosen any tension in the muscle.

4 Continue the kneading on the thigh, working over the top and outside areas with alternate hands. While the leg is still raised, do some soothing *effleurage* (firm strokes) up the back of the leg from ankle to hip. Repeat steps 1-4 on the other leg.

5 Kneel up and pummel your hips and buttocks, using a clenched fist and keeping your wrists flexible.

INVIGORATING OILS
Many oils have a tonic effect, restoring vitality without over-stimulating. As a group, the citrus oils are good for this purpose, ranging from the more soothing mandarin to the very refreshing lemon oil.
Have a warm but not too hot bath, with 4 drops mandarin and 2 drops orange or 4 drops neroli and 2 drops lemon. Alternatively, just add a couple of drops of any of these oils to a bowl of steaming water and gently inhale for 10 minutes, to lift your spirits.

MUSCLE FATIGUE RELIEVERS

When your legs and arms become very tired, either through general tension or muscle fatigue, the contraction of the muscles can lead to poor circulation to the extremities. This can become a vicious cycle, as the restricted blood flow fails to nourish the muscles adequately, leading them to stay in a more contracted state. One or two simple stretches can help to restore blood supply to the area, as well as relieving tight, cramped muscles.

CALF STRETCH

Sit on the floor with one leg out in front of you. Lean forwards and grasp the foot with your hand. Pull the foot gently towards you, feeling the tightness in the calf. If you are unable to hold the foot in this position, try doing this stretch with the leg slightly bent. Repeat with the other leg.

HAMSTRING STRETCH

Lie down flat, with one leg raised and the other knee bent. Stretch the muscle by pulling gently towards the chest. Relax, then repeat with the other leg.

48

CALF AND FOOT EXERCISE
Sit on the floor with both legs straight out in front of you, then alternately flex and extend each foot.

FINGER PULLS
Squeeze each finger joint between your finger and thumb. Then hold the base of each finger and pull the finger gently, sliding your grip up to the top of the finger in a continuous movement.

COLD INFUSED OIL OF LAVENDER
Fill a jar with lavender heads and cover with sunflower or grapeseed oil. Allow to steep on a window-sill for a month, shaking the jar every day. Strain and bottle.

Massage into a stiff neck or back. This oil can also be added to the bath to encourage relaxation. Similar oils can be made from marjoram or rosemary, although the latter should be avoided by pregnant women.

Right: Home-made infused oils are effective and easy to make.

CAUTION
If someone has sensitive skin or suffers from allergies, then try massaging with just 1 drop of essential oil per 20 ml/4 tsp of base oil at first to test for any reaction. Seek medical advice before massaging a pregnant woman.

BACKACHE RELIEVERS

The most common cause of lost time at work is backache. In the great majority of cases, back trouble is the result of chronic tensions which build up in the back. The stretches shown here, based on Yoga postures, are intended to aid flexibility of the spine, and should be performed gently and slowly, all the time breathing deeply.

LOWER BACK STRETCH

1 Lie on your front, with your arms bent so that your hands are directly under your shoulders, palms down.

2 Slowly lift your head and push down on your arms to help raise your trunk. Exhale as you raise your body.

3 If you can, tilt your head backwards and stretch up and back as far as possible. Hold briefly, then relax and lower your body back down. Repeat steps 1–3.

LOWER BACK TWIST

1 Sit on the floor with your legs straight out in front of you.

2 Bend one leg and place the foot on the floor across the other knee.

3 With your opposite arm, reach around the bent leg to catch hold of the straight leg, then twist your body. Repeat on the other side.

SIDE STRETCH

1 Stand with your feet shoulder-width apart and your arms stretched out to the sides.

2 Bend down to one side without twisting your body, letting the opposite arm rise in the air.

3 Stretch the raised arm, look up and hold. Slowly straighten and repeat on the other side.

CHEST HUG

1 To complete this sequence of exercises, relieve any strain in the back by lying on your back with legs bent up and hands clasped around the knees.

2 Lift your head and hug your legs into your chest, hold, then relax. Take care not to strain your neck when lifting your head.

CAUTION
If you have suffered a back injury or have back pain, seek medical advice before doing these stretches. Always stop any exercise immediately if you feel acute discomfort.

CALMING ANXIETY

Anxiety can produce many symptoms, including palpitations, sweating, irritability and sleeplessness. If it continues, it will deplete vital energy, leading to a general state of nervousness and tension. Tense muscles in the face can be released with a gentle face massage, especially using soothing strokes on the temples and forehead.

FACIAL MASSAGE

1 Starting in the centre of the forehead, make small circles with your fingertips, working outwards to the temples. Repeat three times.

2 Use your fingers to gently apply pressure to the area where the eye socket meets your nose. Repeat three times.

3 Move your fingers outwards along the brow bone from the top of your nose. Repeat five times.

4 Starting either side of your nose, move your fingers outwards using circular motions along the cheekbone to the jaw. Pay particular attention to the jaw area. Repeat five times.

For a calming face massage, make up a blend of 4 drops lavender and 2 drops ylang ylang in a light oil such as sweet almond, grapeseed or coconut. Always patch-test a new oil before using on your face.

LIFTING DEPRESSION

Depression illustrates the connection between body and mind: physical and emotional energy are both depleted when you are in a depressed state. Both will benefit from a healthy diet with plenty of raw, vital foods, nuts, seeds and B vitamins. A multivitamin and mineral supplement may be useful until you feel energetic enough to prepare good food. Also try to cut down on stimulants, such as caffeine, which tend to exhaust both body and mind.

UPLIFTING BATH OIL
For a strong but relatively short-lived effect, try 4 drops bergamot and 2 drops neroli essential oils in the bath, ideally in the morning. For a gentler effect, you could use either of these oils – one drop at a time – in an oil burner, to pervade the atmosphere all day long.

RESTORATIVE HERBAL TEA
Mix equal parts dried St John's wort, wild oats and damiana. Put 10 ml/2 tsp of the mixture into a pot. Add 600 ml/1 pint/2½ cups boiling water. Allow to steep for 10 minutes and then strain. Drink one cup slowly, three times a day.

Above: Have an invigorating shower to help you face the day.

Above: Tea made with a mixture of herbal tonics will restore the health of your nervous system, while having a slightly stimulating effect.

IMPROVING SELF-WORTH

Affirmations are a deceptively simple but effective device that anyone can use. Try to use them while in the meditative state, having previously planned and memorized the affirmations you wish to make. We all have attributes and qualities in which we can take pride and pleasure. Emphasize these positive aspects to allay the doubts that only serve to limit your potential. Affirmations can change the way you think about yourself and the way you act and react.

AFFIRMATIONS

This technique requires you to say to yourself, out loud, a positive statement about yourself as you wish to be. To make affirmations effective, they should:
• be made in the present tense;
• be positively phrased;
• have an emotional reward.

Yours is the most influential voice in your life, because you believe it! Be aware of any negative statements you regularly make about yourself – "I am shy," "I lack confidence," "I get nervous when…" and so on – they are self-limiting beliefs that you are reinforcing each time they slip into your conversation. You can use affirmations while meditating to change those beliefs.

• I like my (physical attribute).
• I am proud of my (attitude or achievement).
• I love meeting people – they are fascinating.
• My contribution is valuable to (name person).
• I am lovable and can give love.
• Others appreciate my (opinions, assistance, a personal quality).
• I enjoy being a unique combination of mind and body.

Imagine yourself speaking to colleagues, your boss, employees or friends…See yourself behaving and looking confident, standing and looking like a confident person…Notice how you stand…your facial expression…hear the way that you speak… slowly, calmly, quietly and clearly.

Above: Improving your self-worth will enable you to fully enjoy the company of loved ones.

Right: Value yourself and your positive features.

GETTING A GOOD NIGHT'S SLEEP

Sleeplessness is a common response to stress, as your mind and body refuse to let go enough to give you the rest you need. The resulting disturbed and restless night leaves you more prone to stress and anxiety, and a vicious cycle can be created. Learning to relax has to be built into a daily pattern based on a healthy diet, regular exercise and a calming routine to wind down before bedtime.

SLEEP ENHANCERS

It is important to reduce your intake of stimulating drinks such as tea or coffee, and to avoid eating late at night. Instead, drink a tea made from relaxing herbs in the evenings. A couple of drops of lavender essential oil on the pillow may help, or you could try sleeping on a hop pillow.

It is also helpful to create a relaxing ritual to prepare for falling asleep, with a pleasantly warm evening bath to which you have added a blend of sedative essential oils. Just experiencing a fragrance that you enjoy will help you to unwind. A couple of relaxing blends, without over-sedating, are 4 drops rose and 3 drops sandalwood or 5 drops lavender and 3 drops ylang ylang.

SLEEPY TEA

Put 5 ml/1 tsp each dried chamomile, vervain and lemon balm into a pot. Add about 600 ml/1 pint/ 2½ cups boiling water. Leave to steep for 10 minutes. Strain and drink one cup after supper. Warm the rest and drink before going to bed.

Left: A good night's sleep is one of the best cures of all.

A GENTLE WAVE

These massage strokes wash over the limbs in outward flowing motions, creating a gentle stream of movement. The soft, downward strokes have a hypnotic and sedative effect, and brief pauses in the motion create a lovely, wave-like feeling. Repeat each movement up to five times on each part of the body.

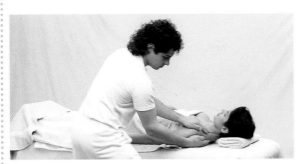

1 Place one hand over the chest, and the other over the back of the shoulder. As you breathe in, pull your hands steadily outwards and down to the edge of the shoulder. Pause briefly as you exhale, lightly cradling the top of the arm.

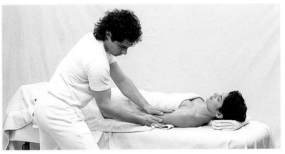

2 Continue the pulling motion down the length of the arm. As you breathe in, pull both hands down to just below the elbow joint. Relax as you breathe out, then continue the slide down the forearm and below the wrist.

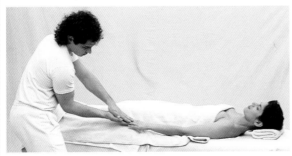

3 Draw your hands over both sides of your partner's hand and fingers, taking your stroke out beyond the body as the hand settles back on to the mattress. Repeat steps 1–3 on the other side of the body.

4 Pull your hands down over the hips and down the leg to just below the knee. Continue this wave-like motion down the lower leg to the ankle, then pull gently and steadily out over the toes. Repeat this sequence of strokes on the other side of the body.

REVITALIZING THE LIBIDO

Tension, anxiety, worry, depression – all these can affect your sexual energy and performance.
Sometimes this leads into a negative spiral of anxiety about sex, leading to less enjoyment and so on.
It is vital to take a little time out of your hectic life to be with your partner and have fun together.
Take turns to massage each other.

HERBAL REMEDIES

Sexual functioning may become difficult because your
energy is too low, or you have a hormone imbalance.
Damiana stimulates both the nervous and hormonal
systems. Vervain releases tension and stress. Wild oats
and ginger are stimulating.

ENERGIZING TEA

Put 5 ml/1 tsp dried damiana and 5 ml/1 tsp dried
vervain into a pot. Add 600 ml/1 pint/2½ cups
boiling water. Leave to steep for 10 minutes. Strain
and flavour with honey. Drink two cups a day.

ESSENTIAL OIL BLENDS

• 5 drops rose and 5 drops sandalwood
• 5 drops jasmine and 5 drops ylang ylang
Use whichever of these blends appeals most to you
and your partner and blend into a base massage oil
such as sweet almond, or create an appropriate atmosphere in the bedroom by burning it in a vaporizer to
sensually scent the room.

Right: Relaxation is an essential prerequisite
to sensuality.

SENSUAL MASSAGE

Take time to create the right environment for this soothing massage: make the room extra special, perhaps play some of your favourite music and have soft lighting or, better still, use candle-light to set the mood. Use soft, thick towels to cover the areas of the body you are not massaging, and make sure that the room is warm, perhaps with an additional portable heater.

1 Place your hands on either side of the spine, but not on it, and glide down the back. Move out to the sides and up the back again. Repeat several times.

2 Kneeling beside your partner, stroke down the centre of the back with one hand following the other smoothly, as if you were stroking a cat.

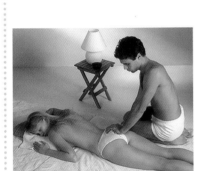

3 Use a firm, steady, circling action on the buttocks.

4 Stroke up the back of the legs, one hand following the other. As one hand reaches the buttocks, start on the calf with the other.

5 Turn your partner over and stroke up the front of the legs, from the ankle to the knee, then from the knee to the thigh.

Stroking movements should be the mainstay of a sensual massage. Use a little more oil than usual to help the hands flow more easily.

REDUCING OFFICE TENSION

For people who spend their working day sitting at a desk, whether at home or in an office, it is very easy to get stiff and aching muscles. As we get tired, our posture suffers and we can find ourselves becoming round-shouldered. Try these simple stretches while sitting at your desk.

1 Link your hands together, palms away from your body, and push your arms straight out in front of you. Hold for a few seconds, relax and repeat.

2 Link your hands together behind your back, over the top of the chair, and lift your arms slightly. Push away from your body, hold, then repeat.

3 Stretch your arms straight out to the sides. Alternately flex and extend your hands, feeling the pull on the upper and lower sides of your forearms.

4 Bend forwards and clasp your ankles. Arch your back to stretch, relax and repeat.

5 Sitting upright, lift and straighten each leg alternately. Flex the foot to stretch the calf muscle. Repeat a few times.

7 Finally, link your fingers together and stretch your arms high above your head.

6 Slowly turn your head from side to side, feeling the extension in the neck muscles.

Many office chairs are not good for the posture, and long hours spent staring at a computer screen can give your neck, upper and lumber back muscles a very hard time. Regular breaks help: get up and walk around every now and then.

PREPARING FOR A STRESSFUL EVENT

If you are getting ready for an important event in your life, you are bound to want to be sure that you will cope well. If you are revising for exams or some other major test, you will need to be able to concentrate when you are working, but also be able to switch off and rest when you stop.

Above: Worrying over examinations is a common cause of stress.

DIET

As well as paying special attention to your diet, you might take a multivitamin supplement or yeast tablets to nourish your nervous system with plenty of Vitamin B. Eat porridge for breakfast every morning. A course of ginseng capsules for 3 weeks before the event will give you energy and help concentration.

Try to take regular exercise, and release the build-up of tension with a relaxing massage or indulgent scented baths.

SUSTAINING TEA

Boil 5 ml/1 tsp each dried licorice and ginseng root in 600 ml/1 pint/2½ cups water for 10 minutes. Pour this decoction over 15 ml/3 tsp dried borage. Allow to steep for 10 minutes. Strain and drink one cup, hot or cold, three times a day.

Above: Vitamin supplements can be useful, but do not make them a substitute for a nourishing, balanced diet.

VISUALIZATION

Visualization requires that you imagine yourself in a situation, behaving, reacting and looking as you would wish to do. Imagine what that will mean for you, your reactions and the reactions of those around you. Feel all the good feelings that you will have when this happens in reality.

It is like playing a video of the event, from the beginning to the perfect outcome for you. Should any doubts or negative images creep into your "video", push them away and replace them with positive ones. Keep this realistic.

Once you are happy with the images you are seeing, note the way you are standing and presenting yourself.

Then allow yourself to view the scene from inside your imagined self. Now you can get in touch with the feelings and attitudes that make the event successful. The best time to do this is when you are relaxed mentally and physically – during meditation. Teach yourself to expect positive outcomes.

The visualization can be combined with affirmations, to make it doubly effective:
• I am quietly confident in meetings.
• I speak slowly, quietly and confidently so that others listen.
• My contribution is wanted and valued by others.
• I enjoy meetings, as they bring forth new ideas and renew my enthusiasm.

Above: The moment of initial introductions can be tense, but remember how you looked, stood and felt in your visualization.

Above: The preparation was worth it: having given your best, you feel good about your performance.

INDEX